I0154932

Sea Dreams

by John Mc Guckin

John Mc Guckin

Original title
Sea Dreams

Cover design
Sonja Smolec

Layout & graphics
Sonja Smolec, Yossi Faybish

Published by
Aquillrelle

Copyright 2011
All rights reserved - © John Mc Guckin

No part of this book may be reproduced or transmitted in any form or by any means, graphic, electronic, or mechanical, including photocopying, recording, taping, or by any information storage retrieval system, without the permission, in writing, from the publisher.

ISBN 978-1-4478-2030-7

Table of Contents

Sea Dreams

4

dedications:

— to my beautiful daughters - Karen, Joanne and Emma, to my wonderful grandchildren - all seven of them, to my former wife - Geraldine, the one who put up with me for 25 years, and to Brian, my big brother,

— to my dear friends Joe Rafferty, the humble man, and to Maggie Kerr from far-away Australia, the lady with a beautiful mind,

— to Mr. Noel Maguire, for his fair and honest critique, to Pat and Michelle Schreuder, my wonderful friends, to Essie Dodds of Castleblayney, and to Josie for the most fun I had having a poem critiqued,

— to the ladies of the Anglicare shop in Hornsby and all the ladies who give their time in Op Shops throughout the world,

— to my publisher Aquillrelle, for their honesty and reliability in their dealings with everyone,

— and a special dedication to wee Liz, the wonderful lady who taught me about life and love, sadly passed away 25th July, 2004 - God bless and watch over her always. Sweet wee Liz - your spirit lives on in all who loved you. "Until we meet again" - forever in love...

Sea Dreams

Rose in Plain Sight

Beneath the heather
Lies a golden treasure
Dormant now that winter's here,
But come the summer

That treasure will flourish and
Give joyous pleasure to all who witness -
The yellow rose.

Purplish-pink may the heather be,
Nature, oft times a shrew can be.
Though a yellow rose

One single, dominant splash
Of golden light,
Lets all who see its perfect form
Gaze in great delight.

And why, because
Nature once again has spoken.
Here, in this heather
A stranger is welcomed
Among its kith and kin,
Regardless of colour - nature nurtures.

Chasing Dream Wraiths

Slipping off to sleep,
Hoping for a peaceful night,
No dreams to disturb my slumber

Allowing tranquility
Full rein throughout the night;
Give me the freedom of sleep

Folded into foetus shape
I pass the night away.
Guarded by angels

Their sentinel forms hold sway,
Throughout the night, no demons
Can attack, my guardian
Angels on full alert

I sleep, I awake, I rise and bathe
Knowing my guardian angel
Chased the dream wraiths away

I Like Me... Being Me

A mind, like a solar system, can be understood by a few,
The world can see what you tell them, but is it the real you?
Always being what you want them to see
You're as sick as your secrets, that's what they tell me.

Beautiful girl, with a lovely heart,
Sometimes the mind can tear that apart.
Living as best as God wants me to be
But unanswered troubles can always haunt me.
To be content and serene, not a lot to seek,
Head troubles take over, and a little pain can leak.

Live without hurting and always be there,
Don't hold on to troubles, they're better to share,
A child God made and in a unique way
Not always perfect, but trying not to stray.

Be the best you can be, and that's how I go,
People who I love the real me, they know.
Don't try to understand me, just love me they say,
Thank God for this statement, I like it that way.

by Michelle Schreuder

Cave

Cave hill - famous, familiar because of its
Nickname Napoleons' nose, sits atop
Ben Madigan, stares across at his distant
Cousin, Ben Nevis, conjoined by strata, though
Destined never to reach out and be friends.

They will never let one another down gazing
Into Belfast Town, Cave hill indomitable still
Watches all the foibles of his minions below,
Their faults he cannot fix, though wonders
Can they not change all the power of minds and
Legs, sadly he thinks they'll always remain this way
They, like him, are conjoined yet apart in mindsets.

His portals always remain open. Mortals pass
Through, and watch the sea as he has for centuries
Thinking, the sea changes, can they not understand
Nothing is steadfast in their short lifespan he is held
In bondage, and often cries silently, tears of rain
Run down into Belfast Town as Cave hill
Watches an old familiar place destroyed by folly.

Enniskillen

Orange or green,
We can all wear the red
In honour of our glorious dead.
An inglorious atrocity
Acted out in
Proud Rosalind's name.

Left only shame
And bewilderment
The wearing of the poppy red
Dishonoured on Remembrance Day.

That inglorious act
Carried out in '87
Shall live forever
In ignominy.

Eleven dead - could the murderers
Not see proud Rosalind's dead
were being honoured there?
Many orange and green died
Upon Flanders' fields.

This atrocity dishonored
Our grandfathers, uncles
Fathers and mothers,
Acceptable collateral.
Can anyone accept
Such a heinous phrase
To try and justify the injustice?

Would they have once again
Used the phrase 'acceptable collateral'?
No one shall claim in Ireland's name,
Be they orange or green

That any action that
Terrifies the populace
Is an acceptable act.
Especially one when we honour
our young, lying dead
In a foreign field.

What right have these cowardly men
To take even one life?
Would that we could
Sweep all these cowards
Aside, and proudly
Wear the poppy red with
Carson and Redmond's men.

So - God's Got a Plan

Explain his plan, go on, explain,
I can't. Why not? I don't understand God.
Then how do you figure he's got a plan?
Look around bunch of no good dumbbells
Hoping God's got a plan.

One that you don't understand, yes, okay, okay,
I'll walk your road, just a little bit and see
What happens. Tell you what, hear my plan,
Maybe he doesn't have a plan, this god you don't understand.

Let's hope he jumps out and says okay, here's the plan,
It's one you don't need to understand.

Let's call all that happens acceptable, and here is
The crux of the plan, all you do is accept that
Where you are at this moment in time is
Exactly were you are supposed to be:- sounds
Dumb to me but then, who am I to understand?
You're this god bloke's friend and hedge
My bets here, we'll call it your plan, alright.

Deserted Britain

Hello, hello anyone there? We're out
In this desert, need a bit of help, hello,
Nobody's there. Has to be, it's Westminster
You're calling. Okay you try Mr Cameron
Are you there? Mr. Clegg, how's about you?

Hello, this is the janitor, who! The janitor!
What are you doing there, cleaning up the mess?
Is anyone else there such as decision making people?
Don't be silly, they're on holiday, Clegg's in Davos,
He forgot that he's in charge as bad as Blair's lot.
Ah we're sort of stuck in the middle of an uprising.
Place called Libya. Libya, heard of it, wouldn't want to be there.

Ere thing is neither do we. O, is that the place Hunt is
Sending the SAS all very hush hush. Of course
Told me, I'm the janitor. Clean up the mess around here.
Let's see there's an old frigate at sea but Hunt forgot,
He's in charge skiing, you see. Very important you lot,
Hang in there, the Captain of the frigate got a lot of sense

Not suffering fools gladly told me, and remember I'm
The janitor. He's going in to get people out. O, just heard Clegg,
And that other guy what's his name, Cameron! Rushing
Back from holiday. Better get back to work. Clean up this mess.
It's been really nice talking to you, take care in that desert now.

It Happened

We caused it to happen through hard work and
Dedication, now is our time to celebrate, take this time
To laugh, smile and seize the day, this moment
In time when we accept victory over selfishness
Is always to be cherished and nurtured.

Simpler in time of adversity to have walked away,
Never looked back. What then? We would always
Regret we weren't strong or selfless enough to help a lover,
Their pain not our pain, their suffering not our suffering, though when
In love our partner's pain and suffering are part of who we are.

Then is when we must be the best we can be, and carpe diem.
And now, now that we stayed, fought the fight of life and gained victory
Lift up your heart, smile, cry, laugh and celebrate, this is our day,
One word sums up the reason for being joyous: OURS, not me, not I,

But instead it's US gaining a worthwhile victory over adversity.
Yesterday is gone now and tomorrow has not arrived, all we
Need is our happiness, on this day we can say: WE were there.

Accessory

Accessory to what - life?
What life, you call this a life,
When I look around what do I see?
Nothing, that's the American dream,
A whole bunch of nothing, fools' gold.

We came into the cities, bought into the dream,
Became an accessory to capitalism, it handed over
A nightmare, we were chasing the will o the wisp
Told no end in sight to our dreams, now staring down
The years at the ruins of life we realise - all lies.
Nowhere to go, all ends here, an American dream
R.I.P.

We're an accessory to radical evil, unnoticed by
'The people', the banks' diversity took the dream and I,
Cast aside, only an accessory, bit of bling - useless.
Our cities and our American dreams lie in ruins.
No now in sight, we are the lost and found
Here we remain an accessory to the American dream.

Through the Lens

Open the lens, peer at any scene -
Through one turn of the lens our perspective on life
Becomes distorted, reality is often hidden
If not completely untrue. The lens
Can ripple into fractures, it is often courted
As factual, should we believe what we see?

Many factors cause us to accept what we see as truth.
Not thinking any mirrored image can change the way we live.
Ignoring that truth's subtle rippling reflects shadows,
That it enhances and changes our perspective on an issue.

Looking through that infernal lens the truth bends,
It becomes what the lens wants us to see.
We watched the last years of prosperity unravel,
The cameras caused a ripple on life that we trusted.

We adjust to deceit as truthfulness. Shall we put away our camera?
Better still - let's open our minds to reality,
Ask and demand the truth as seen through our lens on life.

Empty the Cupboard

Me, why me, I'm OK, doing good,
In fact if you really watch me you'll
See everything is okay with me, never say
Or do anything rude at least don't think so.
I'll empty the cupboard, and have another look.

Bet you I shan't find any old can of beans, if I do
Then I'll empty them out and take a look.
Do you believe I need to empty the cupboard?
I've taken a look in there many a time, haven't seen
Or thought there was anything needed discarded
Although it's been awhile since I had a look,
The cupboard is emptied out, counted the beans.

When I emptied that cupboard - boy, did I get a shock,
Not doing so good, seen myself as others see me...
Glad now I emptied the cupboard and had a good hard look,
Don't want to throw away all the old cans, some of them
May have gone green, maybe hold on to them, but I
Realized the need to empty the cupboard and look inside
Once in a while.

Why, and Yet Again - Why?

Okay, Okay, picture this - you are working,
People are talking and mentioning this mythical
Bloke saying he is good, he is kind, he knows what
He is doing and you, tending a dying child looking skeptical
Wonder - can they not see before their very eyes
This mythical figure they adore doesn't give a damn?

A child has just died in my arms, am I supposed to thank
This mythical figure they all exhort when in pain? All I can see
Is another innocent gone from this world.
My despair is of hopelessness,
So many months I looked after many such as he...

Yet this mythical figure
These people adore, I abhor.
How can a benevolent guy let a child die.

Now I have, an eejit imploring me,
Telling me God knows what he is doing.
Okay so do I, and if that mythical figure
was about, a good kick up the arse
Is where I would start.

Do not talk to me about your mythical God.
Hold a dying child in your arms
Then implore his pity.
You'll see he doesn't give a damn.

A Silence Stained

If we can't leave a note
In the silence
Of people's minds
It seems to me a life unfilled.

In the never ending blare of
This media world
Don't you think it's time,
Good and true men/women
Rent aside the hype?

Wrote our way into
The silence of politicians' minds.
Ask them to speak out
Against injustice everywhere.

Not difficult to listen,
We hear the silence
Every time a politician speaks.

He talks about walking
Side by side though when we do
All we hear is silent speeches.

Don't you think it's time we spoke out,
Asked our politicians
To walk the line and
End the silence in their minds?

Where are we in this wretched world
Stained by deceit?
Ask for justice in your corner
Of this vast world, you will Hear
That evil sound of silence.

We are the workers
Asking the silent blare of
Media hype to end.
I believe in love, peace.

Justice exists in the silence
Of good people's minds everywhere.
Write, and destroy the silence.

Never Fading

The true friends we have in life
Are to be likened to a flower that
Shall never fade away.

That perennial steadfastness
There, to depend upon everyday,
Oft times we accept and do not give thanks

Forgetting that a true friend is a guardian angel.
Through joy, hurt, pain and death, the comforting
Cadence from their voice never fades.

On this day, the only one we have, say I appreciate you
And give thanks to whomever God you love
That never once did you say to him - He's worthless,
And simply walk away.

In our stormy times and hoar-frost filled days,
There is always a lighthouse guiding us to safe harbour

And beneath that hoar-frost covered ground, lies
Always the flower of life that never dies.

That flower is simply known as friendship that
Never fades away.

to Tony Kieran and Geraldine, his perennial flower of many years

Full Circle

Nearly there, the wheel spins slowly,
Gently turning, we cannot stand at rest
Whilst the wheel turns full circle.
Shall we look back in wonder or despair?

This life we live is decided by our actions.
Can we say I did alright, did good, did badly?
Each cycle, how we spent it reflects through
Friendships or affections garnered by our actions.

Can we say - here, take my hand, gave all we had,
Our love or protection, maybe we ignored people?
At the end of the circle we start a new beginning.
Let's hope by our actions we are accepted, in heaven.

Silent Listener

Words swirl all around though
No one's listening. Busy putting their point
Of view across they cannot hear, nor do they
Really wish to know what is
Being expressed by their friends.

Off to the side I espy the silent listener,
Always quiet, always listening, trying to cut
Into the hubbub of conversation then drawing
Back when he/she realizes it's pointless, no one's listening;
Only talking, emptiness expressed in their point of view
Talking aimless inanities shamelessly boring
Though believing they are scoring points by interrupting you.

Then the silent listener realizes he can talk to someone who's
Always listening, even sometimes suggesting actions,
In his quiet way the silent listener hears the words
And knows there is one who is there to turn to.

He may not understand this, all he needs to do is accept
That the man who really talks is also the silent listener.

Do You Mind?

Guess you don't mind if we shower
You with missiles, you do mind?!
You'll find no one who speaks out for the oppressed,
The world doesn't care as long as they can't feel
Your pain, their apathy says - after all you deserved it,
Whatever it is, doesn't matter it's just because we can.

Think we got here by giving a damn such as asking -
Do you mind? Especially people
Who believe they own the land we invade
Now. Where were we?... o yes, going to destroy you.

All we have to do for approval is utter the mind blowing
Term 'the people' understand, then we can huff and puff
Blow your homes down, the world will utter brief cries of
Lament such as, O my God! watching your homes topple down.

But we are America, Saudi Arabia, Germany and England
And you do as we say, why? because we are benevolent,
At Christmas we will send you Santa in a gunship.

His sleigh spewing forth his presents of oppression and
You can give thanks for your Child's gift: maimed, blinded, dying.
We realize you are thankful for the poverty caused by your
Surrender to the winds of power, after all - we know you don't mind
That we misused our power, and invaded your home land.

The Simple Truth?

It's true, I read it in the paper.

Heard it on TV.

Must be true... Isn't!

We're told - this is true, believe!

We need to ask - who are you?

Why should we believe?

All the truths down the years

Are shown to be untrue.

Where is the simple truth?

Hidden, in a beguiling web of lies.

Lies parading as truth. Political hype.

How can we perceive the simple truth?

Answer - we cannot!

No Memories

All photographs removed, all memories
Severed, any reference to the past hidden
Deep within an old chest of drawers,
Let's not give credence to lives once lived.
Laughter, loud and raucous, that once rang true.

Those time are gone, bury them deep in regretful
Minds, don't take them out, you might remember
All those good times, good people best forgotten now,
Only clutter spread around a dead room that we once
Called the living room, sit in silence,
Let the television do your living, and remembering.

Bundoran to Alabama

Decided to go to Bundoran,
Got in the motor car, you know,
One of those things with four wheels
Set off and ended up on an aero-plane.

You know, another one of those things
With wheels and wings heading to Alabama.
How we got from Belfast, starting point, to
Bundoran then ending up in Alabama

God only knows. All we know - it's hotter than
Bundoran, got the start of the town right, capital B,
Thought it's Birmingham England, that's were we should be,
Not Birmingham Alabama.

Gotta start looking for another of those things
With wheels and wings called aero-planes, get us back to
Where we started, think that was Belfast, lots of

B's floating through, only thing is we
Don't got the B we want, that B
Is somewhere over there,
Wherever there is.

Get this thing with wheels to take us to castle bar
At least we will end up in some place with another B
To its name, getting tired of all this bull
There's another one of those B's

Got an idea, lets go back to the B we started
From, that's Belfast, maybe we'll know where
In the hell that B is.

Dedicated to Joe, think we will call him the
Man from God knows where.
Wouldn't do to think of him
As the man with capital B to his name.

Mary Watts

It's sad, we are getting old, Mary.
But you know this hair may be grey now
Though my heart is still as fair as
On the day I first met you, and my love
From then it belonged to you, Mary.

Now as I sit and remember
Those days we wandered and
I held you in my arms
My lovely Mary, I miss your kiss.

Those days of yore may now be passed, Mary,
But to me you are always the dancing girl
I lightly held in my arms and swirled around
Our dance hall of dreams, my lovely Mary Watts.

You will always stay my one love
As I remember days we enjoyed the
Beauty of the sunsets.
Mary you will be forever young.

As I close my eyes and
Drift off into this endless sleep
You shall not hear my voice:
I loved only you, Mary Watts.

Who Do We Really Know?

Do you know me or who
You are? Do you know you?

Difficult to know ourselves, I know,
I can tell lies to myself so how do
I get to know me, or you, we rarely
Listen to ourselves nor do we hear

The speech of empty words from the
People we should know, who do we
Really know, I won't let you in.

Wouldn't do, no, not at all to let you in
And you get to know the real me. How
Could I cope if you told me, I really
Do know you, the truth is better hidden.

I can kid myself I'm a nice guy
Truth is elusive can be true one
Minute falsehood the next moment,
I don't know me, or you, the truth is - at
This moment I don't want to know me, or you.

Fitting In

Who said we have to fit in?
In to what, how other people live?
Follow the crowd, be sheep, give in?

Don't believe in the 'in' crowd.
Me, rather stand on the outside,
Look at all the people trying to fit in.

Seems most people are other people,
Oscar Wilde got that right.
Why it is, most people want to fit in?

Be different, only way at least you're you,
A person in your own right not caring
If you're liked, why worry about fitting in?

Sam Todd for God

Sam TODD for God.

Now many a one
Could agree that poor auld SAM gets
A rough ride in Belfast Town
And I for one wouldn't disagree with ya.

Now Sam's the sort of guy that's been looking
After himself for many a year, but to hear these
Folk in Belfast Town, why, you'd think he's
Just come around.

Tis a queer notion they all have about poor auld SAM
They do declare him a candidate for God
Then there's nowt so queer as folk.

Anyway here we have all these folk practicing
How to be friends with this new kid on the block
Forgetting the like of them hung him on a cross.

Now Sam's the type who forgives and forgets
Unlike this crowd in auld Belfast town.
Why they just damn us all to hell for agreeing
Sam TODD is a likely candidate for God in
Auld Belfast Town.

Let's hear for SAM Todd.

In the wee north any eejit will and doe's declare
I am who I am - Sam TODD for GOD.

Isolationism

We're hemmed in, surrounded,
packed tight, traveling en-mass
no one's speaking or

Reaching out, we're living in a bubble
cast out, ignored, we don't share our thoughts.

People all around, we're apart
living in our oneness

want to speak, can't speak
society won't accept we're a community.

Then I reach out, hello, I'm John,
signing to me a name Angelo,

made deaf by companies' machinery
destroyed my hearing, commerce ruined me,

left me living in isolation
and 'we the people'

have to accept we are living in
Isolationism

Kiss and Tell

Let's kiss and tell about
Franz Ferdinand assassinated in Sarajevo.
The world got a bullet in its head.
Many millions of kisses lying dead since
The Judas kiss that crucified the world.

Did Hitler kiss Eva Braun
Then say let's not tell?
Once again that kiss of death
Bedded down in hell.

Civil rights kissed when sister Rose
Said no, what happened, kiss and tell
Martin Luther King murdered.
kissed by an assassin's bullet.

The black people got civil rights.
Did Kennedy kiss and threaten to tell
Someone said put a bullet in his head.

The inglorious sixties embraced Vietnam.
Another generation didn't get the
Chance to kiss, and tell.

On 9/11 the world towers were kissed
By two planes (many died)
The worlds lost heart, so much kiss and tell
Leading us straight to hell.

Then 'we the people' were courted by
The bankers, again we fell in love.

Kiss and tell, money that's kissed
Is most untrue, better
If the world said - I love you.

Though, think about it,
We would still kiss and tell.
One day, will we watch
Hades and Heaven kiss, and tell?

Positive-One-18

Not a street number though that's what it implies.
Nope, simply the number of places I have lived.
That may seem quite a lot, and to most it is.
Positive outlook needed here - 118 or simply ONE.
Both tell of a life lived, perhaps ONE's steadier than 118.

Moving on becomes an addiction.
Pay the rent, can't, out you go find somewhere.
The carousel of moving on has begun.
Shall I catch a bus with my world safe in a plastic bag?
Maybe a train, could sleep in it. Think: were can I go?

Gotta have a place; get one, try to stay, numbers are mounting.
One becomes 10 then 39, think I'll stop here. What happens?
We have to move on. Suddenly 87 arrived at, good as another.
Keep roaming, 100 arrived at, and I'm still on that carousel.
Ach, well, this life, good, stayed at ONE, bored. 118 is here.
This has to be the road most traveled that hasn't lead anywhere.

One More Time

Say goodbye to love.
One more time I try to recall all the
Silly things said and unsaid, why say
I love you then say I don't love you
Striking out in hurt or embarrassment.

Why not state one more time girl
I love you, leave it alone, enjoy the
Time together, why say goodbye
When each time you want to stay,
Hold her and say sorry, not too hard even
If you are full of self, thinking I'm right.
Even when you are right, you are wrong.

One time when you reach out
She shall have fled forever all because
You thought you were more important.
When you go to sleep alone imagine
Having one more time to make it right
Holding her tight, and saying girl - I love you.

Belfast City

Belfast once a mighty industrial city.
Dormant now, you wait the new dawning.
One who knows you would never deny
Your people toiled from dawn to dusk

Accomplishing the strength that
Makes a city grow in mind and spirit,
The hearts and souls of your people
Standing steadfast with you

Belfast at times is cast as a terrible beauty.
Though in its streets walks a proud people.
People such as half timers who wrought in the mills.
Shipyard men and aircraft builders.

A city divided
Cut in two by the Lagan flow.
One side Co. Down the other Antrim.

Then Divis Mountain with its rivers
Fed the growth of mills,
Now all lie corrosive.

The industry of Belfast disappeared.

Belfast the landfall of its lough
Launched many ships.
Famous and infamous,
This grim city holds all in hock.

Though they have redeemed themselves many times.
Belfast City.
Lying smug in its verdant valley
Playing host to myriad guests

Who visit and exclaim in wonderment
Upon Castlereagh hills,
And Black Mountain whilst
We the people disdain
Our pride of Belfast Town.
This now living City.

Talk to Me

Talk to me
why won't you
talk to me

What did I say
please tell me
talk to me

Can't go on
this way,
talk to me

What future
in silence,
talk to me

Going nowhere with you
can't stand the silence.
Why won't you
Talk to me?

Fundamentalists

In these enlightened medieval days, Iran
Enjoys the weirdness of Islam. The joy of the so
Called prophet Allah. The inhuman beating of women
To death with the male interpretation of the Quran.

Of course the devil himself hides inside the pages.
Declaring women are inferior - inferior to whom?
Some illiterate moron who has been taught to blow
Himself to bits in the devil's name, O sorry, Allah's name.

Not much difference in hell from either,
Woman, hide your shame, you are making this peaceful!
Male wants you. Although why is he so
Lustful of another man's wife?
Did he not learn how to respect women from his prophet?

Only blind obedience to an archaic text that
Is dismissed by any sane person.
Though in Islamic fundamentalist minds

The Quran says it all. Blind obeisance to Allah
Expect respect, and obedience from women.
Who are these men, do they believe in love or lust?
Women, hide your body, there's a male about.

Change

Change is akin to pushing water uphill.
Wanting things to remain the same, but
Always events flow around, bewildering at times
Then, everything slows to normal and why,
Because we plugged the dam of our emotions.

Not adverse to change, accepting
Why I decided it was time for change,
Needing to pay attention
To the tenet that change
Only comes from within, and as long
As I remain true to my emotions.

Change, and the unnecessary feeling
Of pushing water uphill
Can be dealt with, instead of struggling
Let's float as if
In clear pools where
The water has stilled.

Misunderstanding

When you came to this land you said you came to understand.
Soldier, we are tired of your understanding.
Tired of the British troops on our soil. Tired of the rifle butt on the head.
Tired of the knock upon the door. Tired of the jails and beatings.
Tired of the deaths of old friends.
Tired of the tears and funerals, those endless endless funerals.
Is this your understanding?

by Frances Morris, written on a gable in Belfast in the seventies, since painted over

Take My Hand

Take my hand, let me walk you through
This our wondrous land. Hold on tightly.
We are going on a magnificent journey.

Our singular land, one world.
Beautiful in its entirety, many different
People and sights to see, don't let go of my hand.

Though even if you get lost, wait for the stars.
Journey on, guided by nature's many varied landfalls.
Hold on to nature's hand, you can't go wrong.

This land's so strong in its grandeur, North, and South.
We can walk and talk holding on to each other's hand.
Gaze at mountainous ranges, look out upon rainforests.
Even the cities that the world of man has built
Contain many stupendous artefacts.

Let's walk, hold on to my hand, we shall exclaim
In wonderment at each new sighting aware of
Our smallness in this our one world. Created by
Another's hand, one that we cannot understand.

Sea-dreams

Where the earth and sky collide
That's were sea-dreams are found,
Sea-dreams become reality as sunrise
Grows glorious out of aquamarine horizons.

Our dream - that love is all we need,
In our sea-dream moments, looking beyond
Horizons, we see our dreams come true as we
Sway with loves promise in the daylight,

Holding each other, kissing each other
Sea-dreams are a reality that only mystic
Lovers know, dreams happen, and
When they do

We accept that love is
All we need, and
We few who embrace
The might and power of love
Live forever in our sea-dreams.

Fading Away

Watching you fading away from me
Makes me think of all the times we spent apart.
How I wish we had those times back again. Now
I pray that you could stay. Although, looking in your eyes
I know, yes I know, you're at peace, and fading way.

I'll hold you, kiss your loving eyes closed, and murmur a prayer
Knowing in my heart we'll be together again.
Loving one another, we shall not see each other for
Many a year, but I shall hold our memories dear.
In the morning, after the still of the night,
I'll whisper I love you, hearing your final
Words echoing in my mind, it was so good to see you.

Memories will never fade away wee Liz.
Simply become bearable.
I know that tomorrow was promised to no one.
Though, when I awaken each morning, I wish you were there.
Goodbye for now, listen as you gently fade away into the night, and
You shall hear my pray to you, three simple words, I love you.

Art of Life

To survive, art has to be tangible,
Able to state - here I am, touch me,
Caress me, covet me. I'm the art of life.
In my many forms I am sought after,
Despised, copied, and stolen. I am what I am.

The art of life. How you view me is from your
Take on life. That truth remains inviolate.
My sense of being encircles the globe.
Known as imagination, I belong to each one of you

How you pursue me depends on how much of being
You is allowed to shine through. Reach out,
Grasp hold of me, I belong in your mind..

Good, bad or indifferent, use me...
Your imagination decides how I come to life.
I cannot live with you, you are me and I am you.
The art of life.

Reason to Believe

I have reason to be thankful.

Why? Because I have reason to believe in love.
Love is also beyond reason, illogical and magical,
It bestows grandeur on the poorest, majesty on the richest,
Love does not discriminate, love is.

Saying yes when you mean no, or no when you mean no,
The illogical splendour of being in love is unreasonable
Yet, I have reason to believe in love.
I have lived, I have loved, and in my family I find love still.
No need to look for love, it lives inside each of us.
Reach out, embrace the one you are with, you may find
You too have reason to believe in love

The music of love is silent, loud, raucous, and lost in mystery,
That moment when you suddenly raise up your voice and
Say I Love You, and find that you have reason to believe,
Because love is.
There is no other way in the world to live
Than to be in love, and say I Love You.
Try it, grasp the reason to believe.

ATTEN-SHUN!

Atten-shun! at ease!
atten-shun!
You're caught unawares
didn't pay attention.
Stood down, at rest,
let the fat cats feed you tidbits
whilst you lingered at their table
of opulence.

Atten-shun!

We, the CEO'S of the world
own you, body and soul.
We 'arranged' allowed
all of you to kick an own goal
now we are telling you
do as you are told,
we're sweeping aside the mess
you have made of your lives

At ease!

Nothing better than having the
righteous
believe they are in the wrong
and we mighty few who caused
this St Crispin day
shall step forwards, and do as we do

Take! Take! Take!
No welfare state.
Why not? you plead.

Atten-shun!

We need it for our handouts,
give to our needy patrons,
Stand down, you've been told,
We are your CEO's
Of this world.

ATTEN--SHUN!

Danger, High Voltage

Consumer needs encased in steel.
Sign declaring danger misted over
In drizzling rain, obscured by graffiti.

People walking by bowing their heads
Beneath overhanging trees, see not the
Absurdity of nature's sentinel towers guarding
Their consumer needs: Electricity

When nature wants high voltage it strikes
From storm filled skies. Man puny in this
Environment can only cower, and exclaim
"Danger, high voltage."

He cannot encase nature in steel, nor
Cover it in graffiti, his basic needs
Baseless in nature's environment, he can
Only write: Danger, high voltage - Keep Out!

Across the Line

Many lines are so finely drawn
In Belfast town, hard to see the divide,
difficult to know when You have crossed
from one divide into another
Dimension of hate and bigotry.

A name, a place, an incident
spoken in the wrong place
at the wrong time earns You
the eternal right to be killed
in the Unspoken law of bigotry
simply because You strayed

across the line
into our area. That area.
Do you belong in it?
Are you Jewish Catholic,
Hindu Catholic, Protestant Jew
Or Hindu Protestant - it does not matter.

You are not one of us.
Who are we? We are the 'people'
and we hate everyone,
no discrimination, we just hate
all of you. We have huffed,
and we puffed then have blown
your lives away, tortured, slaughtered.

Especially in the romper room
on a pleasant Sunday morning
having a wee drink before church.

Belfast, Belfast, we love our Town,
you are Very welcome as long

as you don't Stray across the line
once you do you'll be lucky, lucky, lucky
if we the people let you leave walking.
Remember this is our Town
don't stray Across the line.

1920 to 2011 still the same hate prevails

Softly Kiss Me Goodnight

Kiss me softly as you stroke my hair
And bid me gently goodnight, sweetheart,
Until the morning I shall hold you tight, and if you
Awaken it will be alright, my comforting arms will keep
You from harm, drift peacefully to sleep my sweetheart.

With the dawning of the new day as you stir awake
I shall be here to kiss you gently, and say
Good morning, I love you my one true and only sweetheart,
Let us seize this day and proclaim to the world our
Love that comes solely from the heart, you are my one love,
Turn to me, let me kiss your lips as I whisper you are beautiful.
On this new day I pledge to you my troth, sweetheart.

Beauty is to be found in the mind, and you are wonderment,
You truly care and look after everyone, that's
The reason why on this new day I will share
With you straight from my heart, I love you
My darling girl, my one true sweetheart.

Night Light

Turn on the light
Let me know you're alright.
Don't turn away,
Give me a second chance.

Can we turn back the night?
Please, let me hold you tonight,
Tomorrow will be too late.
You are my world,
Hold me, turn off the light.

We still have tonight,
Kiss me; tell me it's alright.
Baby, baby, tell me you love me
Why don't you turn off the light
And hold me tight?

Let's Walk

Come on, let's walk and talk,
We'll go down along, by the sea shore,
Paddle as we did when we were kids,
Isn't it great strolling once more
Down by the sea shore, all cares tossed aside
Disappearing into the sunny sky

Come on, run and play, we're all kids once again,
I know, let's built sandcastles right up to touch the sky.
Never, can't do that. Why not? we're kids once again,
Let your imagination fly.

Okay, let's do it, after all we're down by the seashore
All is possible in the imagination of a child.
Come on and play, put away grown up thinking
All and everything is possible when we play
Down by the seashore.

Cup of Tae

A cup of tae you say,
Okay, that'll do, give's it.
What about a biscuit as well.

What? No biscuit, why not?
Need one to dunk in me tae.
It's not messy can't have a cup
Of tae if I don't have me bickie.

I'll cry into me tae, whet's that you say,
Go ahead ye say, give over will ye,
All I want is some quiet time and not
You blathering on about a biscuit with
Your cup of tae.

Authorized

I'm authorized to take your life,
Don't ask who authorized me.
Suffice to say I have the authority.
It's enough that I proclaim I'm authorized.

Thank me, why ask to be spared, look around,
Is this life worth living? Here I am, consider me,
The reaper man, it'll help you accept that I'm authorized.
The eyeless men gave me a gun, sent me on my way,
Called out to me - you're the reaper man - Authorized.

To kill anyone and you are anyone, so there.
You need to know how I got authorized.
Easy, the eyeless men decreed it.
We won't question their,
Authority, even though we elect them.
Shall we ever truly know them when
They are in authority?

Northern Union Blues

I'm telling you there's nothing
The union will do.
You may be in our union but
We don't want you.
On the grip you see,

Only way is, to do as we say.
How do I live, no way your way?
Knuckle the forelock
That's Union ways, not our way.

We are the new breed of working man,
Stand our ground.
Fight for the right to a decent life,
The union man doesn't understand.

We are the UNION. Together we are strong.
Fight for our rights.
Can't, you are hard working men
On the lump we disagree with you.

Northern Union won't tolerate you,
Stand down or stand alone.
We always have said I.

No different now said I.
We work and lose but
Never bow down.
You say we're wrong.

Represent us, no way, said he,
You lot are not union men,
Hard working guys, and we won't
Be a part of you, okay, said I,

We'll walk this road ALONE.
The UNION blues played out.
The only sound we hear said I
Is the defaming sound of silence.

Commodity

I'm a necessity,
Nothing wrong
With my perception
Of my usefulness, after all
We are all here to be used.

It's how we let ourselves adapt
To other people seeing
And needing us as a commodity,
Need we let them buy and sell us?

Our fault we let ourselves
As a person fade from reality,
We make them
Feel good, though it's only when
They feel that it s time we were used.

But that strange old feeling goes on and on,
As I said it's nothing new, everything
Is still the same, I'll keep on keeping on.

Think it's time we worked out
Is this all I am to you?
A necessity perhaps, I'll say.

Well, I don't need you to shoulder my bag,
Wander off to find a life.

Who knows what I'll find, most likely
End up dreaming of you
On another, never ending road.
Goodbye might not be so good,
Perhaps realize I liked being a commodity.

Reach Out

Reach out, give and you will receive
The good in our world of today,
All is good if you reach out, rejoice and
Love one another. Seems so simple yet,
We put demands on the simple act of saying
I love you.

All I ask is for you to stand by me
When I reach out to you, and ask
Do you love me?
An easy question,
Why complicate it,

Yes I love you,
Let me hold you,
Dance with me,
Hold me tight.

Sway to life's music.
Reach out, say it loud
I love you.

Life is contained in these three words.
I love you,
Love lasts for ever.

Through all trials and
Labours of living in this world
Let us reach out.

No one can be an island.
Someday we all will reach out,
Say yes, I love you.
Love you, love you.

Building Blocks

Pour the foundations, build the blocks.
Simplicity itself, no great knowledge needed.
Then we have a home, a City which becomes the
Home of man, and that's when simplicity ends.

We have unknowingly built in egocentricity.
Foundations we poured were strong and true.
The blocks set upon them, tottering now. Falling apart
Because City's ego won't allow judgement upon itself,
Don't Think or look different, Adhere to our plan - Sameness.

Do you think as we do, do as we do, and who are we?
Why, we are the government elected by you to rule.
We make laws, decisions so you can live in comfort.
This City is built on strength of hope and charity won't allow
Free thinkers, only upsets our apple cart, can't allow that.

What was that you said, you want a home, we destroyed
Your livelihoods by our ineptness in shoddy planning,
Couldn't be you elected us, we are you. Only problem is
This great City built on faith, hope, and charity is slipping
Into the apathy of Orwellian minds, we do as we like.
You, the people, i.e. workers - do as you are told.

Equalizer

We are all created equal.
Or so the story goes, then how come some
Think they are more equal than you or me.
Is it because of the gun?
Perhaps concede, they have a point.
Have to consider - is it for good or evil?

Then let's consider that point,
Look at it from different angles.
See how it plays out. Okay let's surmise
Gun doesn't exist. Different story then.

Not so big and strong without a weapon.
Who gave them the gun, were did it come from?
Some say Sam Colt, me I say our minds, inherited
From that God bloke, along with choice.

Maybe need to look further, that God
Fella gets blamed on an awful lot.
Now we got a brain, 'God given' we need to eat.
But, that wee but, causes lots of dissent,
We don't need the gun to feed, to survive.

Can't argue it's for good.
When did good come from killing, maiming?

Government man got the gun, terrorist man
He got the gun.
Ordinary bloke don't want no gun.

But, and again we have the wee but,
Insecure man. He needs the gun.

Now, that God guy who stands for love,
He gets blamed on all the wrongs
In this blighted world.

Now that we have looked at it
From upside down, and inside out,
There is no reason to have a gun.
Let's survive without it.

All those body bags brought
Back from inferior man's killing ground,
Only fodder for his ego.
Reckon it's time we got rid of the gun.
Although many insecure people believe in the gun.

Warning

Warning: video and voice recordings,
We're watching and listening to you,
Nothing you can do that won't incriminate,
We the authorities are on to you.

Watching, always watching, yes, you,
Who - me? haven't done anything, yet.
Neither will you, we the authority,
Have cameras and video recordings.

Everything needed to prosecute,
Yes law-abiding you.
We are everywhere, on the roads, in trains
Buses, planes, and automobiles pretending
To protect you, don't ask what from.

We don't know, that's why we have voice and
Video recordings of you, who me? yes you,
Watching, watching, warning you-be good.
Can't say we didn't warn you, all the signs say
Warning, video, and voice recordings.

Choosing

Ordinary day, my stomach in knots,
old people, places, things calling the shots.
Knowing a way to help get some stillness
but pain keeps coming, making me ill.

A million friends for everyday,
but stubborn or careless that's how I stay.
Few problems shared could still my mind,
but my thinking is off, no answers I find.

This too shall pass, and thank God above,
fear will win if I don't accept his love.
He taught me to learn my faith keeps me strong,
Each ordinary day I keep plodding along.

by Michelle Schreuder

Puppets on a String

On stage of our own making, jerking,
Around 71% of the public voted for me before I
Drifted off down south leaving you our voters
To believe in fairy tales, storybook lies,
Watching you dance on strings of hope.

Then, when the time was right I waltzed off
South of the border, down Fianna Fáil,
Way to become one with their establishment.

After all when on stage and the backdrop burns,
It's all part of the act as we jerk you lot around,
Knowing you are gullible, puppets on a string
Left in despair all you can do is watch as I take flight.

Winging my way south to Louth, you can watch charades
From afar as I gleefully strike body blows on all fronts
And enter into the gubernatorial championship ring.

United in pockets, overflowing with forty piece of euros.
Looking after my egoistical instincts; my sleight of hand
Making it appear that I looked after my adoring public.

All puppets, whilst here I sit laughing in my chair in state
Parliament, conscience eased, after all I didn't take my seat
Under British rule, only their money, and does that count?

Don't think so, you can all dance to the D.U.P. rule, I'm
Your leader of Sinn Fein, do as I like, 71% of rejects
Left behind to fare for themselves under John Bull rule.

No more shall I care, though, never did simply play
The game of jerking the reins to watch you dance like
Puppets on a string, only I win as I fold up my tent and run
Off down south, and there share my perfidy with others of my ilk.

Montage of Love

Memories hidden amid a collection of photos
Not letting anyone know the truth of our love.
The montage tells of a love lost through
Indifference to your emotions, you were my gypsy woman.

What happened to nights when I held you?
And those early morning hellos?
Never told you I loved you. I gaze in deep regret
At loving eyes staring out from
A montage of photos.

Strange, I would like to say new words to you, my
Thoughts stray to you. I never think of those gray
And bad days. I ever only think that I never minded
The rain when I was with you, but like all the good in life
.
You are gone from my life. Even though I believe in love
It was easier to stray, not accept responsibility.
Now I know I need you,
But the page of life is written, and I just
Stare at your loving eyes
lost in the montage of photographs.

Atomic Number (6)

Carbonic, moronic, we need a carbon tax.
These colourless words in Gillardesque drives
Another nail into Australian workers' chronic living
Got a lot of nothing talk, put living back where it belongs
In the workers homes, O, you mean 'those' Voters

Those moronic twelve year olds, who are they?
We need to, I don't know, it just sounds good, carbonise
The workers take their livelihoods, after all we are government
Can't say we're moronic, you voted for us we'll give
Black diamonds with our carbon tax to ourselves.
Leaving you odourless, homeless, we could care less
Just say okay, put the carbonic, moronic tax in place.

Atomic 6 honorific title for an odoriferous tax,
All meaning lost in wording, no sense in trying
To understand content, believe me, we are moronic,
Carbonic politicians telling you what's good for you.
Read about it, you won't understand, I don't, and I'm
Writing moronic, carbonic verses whilst, lmao.

Ireland's Warriors

Let us
Dance, entwined.
Hold me close,
For your love is all.
In your eyes I see love
Though, I know it's not for me.
Your mistress, Ireland,
Has forever ensnared your heart.
That cruel Rosaleen.
On this night of sadness,
Please, hold me tight, let me
Kiss your mistress' eyes.
I know your thoughts,
Lie with her, and tomorrow
Shall be a blood filled day.

Walk Softly Away

Close the
Door softly as you go.
Wander off into the soft night.
Don't look back,
I won't be standing
At the window, I'll listen as
The door closes.

I was always here.
Now I know it was a lot of
Time wasted.
Step softly as you go.
Close the door quietly.

An aura of lies is draped around you,
Go gently into the night.
Let me rage softly against the deceit
In your lying eyes.

I was always surprised
With the look in your eyes
When I said, I love you.

Realized you were only using me.
Walk softly away.
The house is a blank.
A lesson learned. Don't look back
Your insincerity glows.

I shall have all the lights out.
And don't look back.
The house will forever
Be in darkness to you.

Have a Little Faith

A million thoughts for a sensitive mind,
a massive heart looking for kind.
Wisdom is a fountain not always found,
but treasure all you have, plenty going around
Not all of it sounds like good advice.

Challenge each day as precious as can be
Not every moment is promised to me.
If I keep love in my thoughts and peace as a must
my life will be wholesome never turning to rust.

Give others a chance to shine or be frost,
Each are a player and have sometimes lost.
Be yourself and add a little faith within,
Pause everyday you may need to rethink
Though, whilst you retain faith, you'll always win.

by Michelle Schreuder

A Life Less Tearful

There were times when I was happy
But there were too many nights
When I was unhappy loving you, and you
Not there, I wished you loved me.

Living life in sadness hoping for your love.
We should have lived in joy not this tearful way.
If I could turn around go my own way,
I would live a life less tearful far away from you.

Strange, we make our own bed then lie in it alone.
Not wasting more time on you, gonna go my own way.
Same as you, though I won't look for someone new.

Even if I was loved by the best, nobody would earn
My trust again, the best I can do is walk this road alone.
Believing in love, wishing it had been there for me.

Just for Tonight

I'm sitting, drinking sherry.
Thinking I'll get merry.
Pour me another, let me stay mellow.

Show me the door when, if I have too many.
I loved it when you said hello.
In meantime pour me a sherry.
Am I merry already? The room started
Spinning around, okay, I'll go, take the night,
And the sherry, walk down by the shore.
Never been there before, not surprised.

Always been too unsteady, can't blame the sherry
Forgive me, guess the drink has taken hold.
Pour me that sherry, I'll take my mood home
See the shore another time, it's always there
In many beguiling forms, backlit by moonlight
Let me carry that moon home in indigo bottles.

Pour me a sherry, let me stay...
It's only for tonight, I'm free when
I stay in dark bottled light. Don't shout,
Please hold me tight, this is all I have.
Just for tonight let me be merry.

Resources

Road or rail, sea and sky
Movements of goods
Never cease
Fossil fuels wasted
Though goods will move
By road or rail, sea and sky
Resources gone, depleted.
But goods must move
By road or rail sea, and sky
Feeding the stomach of avarice.

Mr. and Mr. Right

Two wrongs do not make a right.
What then do we do when two rights
Are wrong, adopt a passionate sleight
At Noel and Danno for the audacious manner
In which they stated we are right?

These guys are the experts in technology,
Making computers, fixing problems all
Day, whilst here is little
Silly old me, asking them are you sure?
Of course we are, we are Mr. and Mr. Right.

Then, when shown they are wrong, both wrongs
Shrug their shoulders and declare we don't fix TV's
To walls, only advise, and laugh ourselves silly
That you will take our advice.

May I have Microsoft 2011, download Photo Shop5?
Of course, in this matter we know, we are right.

Okay, my fault, next time I go to the horse's head,
And not its ass, as that's where Mr. and Mr. Right belong,
They declare we are right, you are wrong, and we don't care
Because, you should not have asked us - are you right?

Fish and Chip

Fancy a chip, ach, get us a fish
Okay, no problem, only that fateful
Saturday afternoon in '93 there occurred
Another act of Belfast infamy, fish, and chip
Please, asking, as two delivery men brush past

Innocuous in their uniforms, though, blindly carrying
Death, murder, and mayhem into an innocent
Saturday afternoon, their bomb cover tray exploded
Prematurely, killing eight innocent customers, and one
Terrorist, no right, only one dastardly
Wrong on the Shankill road, that 23rd day of October in '93
Innocence's asking for a fish and chip blown into eternity.

What certainty, in evil minds, can condone a savage act?
Rebellion against whom - workers, same people
As they, no justice in their actions, only bloody murder
As all around them innocent people asked, may I
Have a fish and chip please, do you want salt vinegar?
Okay, the reply, and then the premature fireball swept them away.

Mountain Road

Built as a serpentine
The mountainous road
Lets us cling tightly to the
Refuge offered.

Struggling forwards the
Mountain people take
It in their stride striving onwards,
On winding roadway, each step a danger.
In a life of unforgiving poverty,
If you slip no one can help.

No love lost on nature's wonders,
Each footfall a battle, toiling and
Striving to arrive before the sun sets.
Home at last, no matter how dire: Home.
Is the heart's rest: At peace...

Two Out of Three

Two out of three isn't bad, but here
We enter into the dilemma of settling for less,
What has become of one, if two's not okay why have two?

And who are we, to sell ourselves short and accept
Less than three, who told us that two out of three ain't bad?

Let's look at one, okay, here is one, small fella, jobbie
On his own, left to wander around as the bit in the middle
Sometimes known as truth,

Maybe that's why we accept that
Two out of three ain't bad, easier than looking at pitfalls in life.

Drift around those tru-ism leaving one to fend alone.
Let's take back three out of three is best. And two can
Be friends with truth and remember two out of three ain't good at all.

There Were Shadows

Deep down in all our minds
There are shadows twisting and churning,.
Folded into crevasses in the consciousness,
Seemly no structure or substance though, always
There are reasons why we cannot let them surface.

Hiding from self, cannot face the shadowy truths
That we all must one day draw forth and confront.
It's easier to hide in the shadows of our minds and
Twist reality to suit our dishonesty with self.
That moment when shadows roil forth saying - here I am,
Talk to me, deal with me, only way to find your peace of mind.

Always there are going to be shadows in all our minds.
We need to sweep the shadows aside, let them dissipate.
By confronting our fears we find that all the crevasses
Where the shadows lurked are closed and sealed.
Accepting there were shadows that
No longer trouble our minds.

Bag of Hammers

I've been given a bag of hammers
Pondered on where to use them
While pondering I thought I'll knock some sense into people
Looked around
Who shall I start with?

Then looked at myself
Good beginning, I need a thump
When I finished with myself, I left bloodied and bewildered, no wiser.
I thought it would be easier to talk with someone,
I'll go out.

Leave my bag of hammers behind,
Striking out doesn't work
Find a friend, shake their hand
Walk with them awhile, talk with them,
It might work in an easier, softer way.

Belfast Far Away

Seems so distant now
That place called Belfast, standing in
Sydney City thinking home is so far away
Wondering will I ever belong here,

Belfast will always be there,
Lurking in my mind as I think of
Its kindness to people
Be they rich or poor,

The friendly banter in large
And small stores, won't matter
Who you are, where you come from,
Its people
Hear you say something, anything,

They pick up the conversation
Then, the banter starts. Here in Sydney
Only the daily grind, and no one says hello.

That old Belfast town,
A City divided but its people
Seem to be able to leave the politics behind, and simply
Greet you in its City streets

One time in castle junction
I stood and stared at Albert clock,
Belfast's Pisa, and wondered,

Why doesn't it topple over,
After all, built on top of
Farset River, turned away and looked

Down Donegal place
There's City hall built on the site
Of the old linen hall

Looked up at the façade of Scottish provident
In Donegal square west,
Old Belfast industry etched in stone,

Will Future generations wonder?
What happened, all gone?
That's Belfast far away

Honesty

Honesty, simple in terms of saying
'Of course I'm honest'. Though when we
Delve into its complexities, uncertainties
Concerning motives invade our thinking.
In all truth - how honest are we, or need to be?

Society demands we tell the truth, to be honest.
Though, what happens when honesty contains brutality?
Truth and honesty oft times need to be tempered with reality.
In all our dealings with humanity, dignity can be destroyed
By so called honesty, knowingly hurting when the little
White lie would suffice. I tell the truth, O, you are so honest.
Then we can strut about, esteemed for our honesty.

Uncaringly sharing honestly can cause hurt, pain, and despair.
The humanness of people's feelings needs to be considered.
Our honesty - is it malicious? If it is, then do we want it?
That's when the honest answer is better told as the wee white lie.
No hurt is caused, living can go on in peace, and contentment.
Consider your motives in honesty. Are they noble or just gossip?

Bandage Round My Heart

Listening to children talking about
Mommy and daddy fighting, saying
Mommy needs a bandage round her heart,
I would like one, stop hurting in my head.
When mum and dad start shouting, I scream -

Are we always going to live this way,
Dad drinking?
And mom, will she always
Need that bandage?

I can't stand them living this way.
Wish I could run away.
Run away, nowhere to go
Wish I had that bandage,

My head is getting tighter.
Won't, don't want to stop screaming
It blocks out the tears in mommy's heart.

I'll go outside, listen to the wind,
Hear other people screaming
I'm lost in this familiar street.

I know it's home but I can't
Help mommy tie that bandage
Round her heart, it hurts
So bad when I think
They don't love me anymore.

Someone, anyone
Can you tie a bandage
My mommy's brokenhearted,
I'm scared.

Listening to Time

Time can be likened to a teardrop
On the cheek of the world, let's reflect
On old and new moments of time in
Our everyday lives that benefit or enhance
The meek in this beautiful world.

Moments in time we sometimes take no notice of
And miss the beauty of life. A newborn child's cry,
The sound of love is heard if we listen, learn to accept
Any adversity that befalls the child who, in time,
Comes to live in our hearts, listening to
That child lets us hear the sound of love.
In its cries lies the beauty of life.

Welcome winter and summer into your time,
All love filled memories children remember
Give thanks for everyday they spend with you
Lend your moments in time gracefully and
You shall find peace reigning within your mind.

Time is fleeting, and as the teardrop can be
Wiped away so too can happiness.
We all need to live in the day seeking to
Make good use of our lives reaching out
To those we love, and say I love you.

I Forgot

What did I forget, how to laugh?
Most importantly I forgot
How to say no.
No to most of the useless demands
That being married
Heaps upon you,
In the midst of doing things.

You lose sight of yourself,
All you have is a worried mind.
Laughter, an alien sound you hear
and think - I used to do that.
What happened, forgot to laugh.
Just took life too seriously
And started to live a lie.

Not the lie of family.
They are all important, simply
Thinking OK, you want more,
I'll go out and get more.

In today's society we want,
What do we want?
More, that we don't need
And we forget to laugh.

Dickens stated it years ago -
Earn sixpence save
A penny, happiness.
Spend nine pence, unhappiness.

The Wind Has Stopped

The wind has stopped blowing, there is
A sense of stillness in people's minds.
Time to think upon life and all its hardships.
When we let ourselves be blown here and
There by any whim that takes us we forget
Life, and do as we like. We treat life as a waltz,
With all the grief that we have successfully
Cast into the wind - death, sickness, disability.

Our friends were caught up in their cold winds of life
As we blithely went our own merry way riding
That carousel to nowhere. Time now, that the
Wind has stopped blowing, to look around reach out
Our arms give life a hug and help a friend.
Offer to listen, and hold their problems in our hearts.
Offer solace let them know how much we love them.

The winds shall once again blow, and then it could
Be a cold, cold wind with not a friend in your life.
If you let the wind blow you here and there
It becomes so difficult to utter these simple words,
Hello again, I love you, and missed you.

Warriors

Who is right, who is wrong?
In God's mind we all are at fault.
To say God bless our soldiers seems
A travesty of God's love for all of his creations.
Who is right, the one who states he is.

The one who commits the worst atrocities,
The governments who declares we will fight,
The terrorist who declares I'm right and we shall fight,
None of them in God's mind is right. Thou shall
Not kill seems to be a forgotten commandment of all.
Our one God - why do we not demand of governments
To look to our past to see clearly our future?

Shall we forever waste the lives of our young men
And women? Give us peace, this word appears
To breed abhorrence in all our leaders.
Peace in our time, when is it to be?
Never it seems, we waste all
These lives and our egoistical leaders
Bow their heads as the strains of the last
Ring out, ask them then
Do you cry for these young people?
If you do stop killing and maiming,
In God's name - stop!

Demons at Bay

A past so troubled, impossible to erase,
a brand new life with a less worried face.
Demons to haunt you, because of it all,
ready to break you ready for a fall.
Yet destroyed as I was with a nasty addiction
recreating a future this time fiction.
For reality was unbearable and sanity at bay
thank God for the help to see a new day.
Say a few words, thank you creator,
gone are the days of the dark invader.
Never erased always there, the difference today
is no more despair. Your past makes Your future no matter how bad
put it behind you never stay mad.
People who love will love and forgive,
people who can't, in your life no longer they live.
Time is a healer, our demons will remain
however they ease and we bury our pain.

by Michelle Schreuder

God's Chosen Friends

God knows my very soul, who I need near,
That's why he picked friends for each different tear.
He only sends the ones with a special heart.
Those who understand, don't build walls nor tear us apart.

That's why I know you and am glad of his choice,
You can tell when I'm in pain by the tone of my voice,
You never judge and I know that you care,
In life I am blessed as you are always there.

Miles away but that never matters,
You still know if I'm happy or my life is in tatters.
Till he calls us to his home whenever it may be
Thank GOD for the friend, he sent YOU to guide ME.

by Michelle Schreuder

The Roundabout

When I was but a child
I played on the hobby horses
Usually on mild sunny days

Days of innocence that have now run their course
Local Bobbies chased you for playing ball
Never for running and shouting yourself hoarse

Shouts of glee and merriment as we spun
Above the ground on our carousel of gold
Of course we all felt so very, very bold

Playing on the hobby horses not knowing
Or showing fear, after all we were kids
When our mothers called we let on we didn't hear

The clip clopping of the old horse was greeted
With the swelling of children laughing and playing
Only memories remains of hobby horses going round

Along with the local Bobbies chasing children.
No one to lobby for the hobby horses, they died away
And left a deep cleft in the streets of Belfast town
Who would ever have thought the hobby horse would die?

Spirit

Let me touch your spirit.
Life destroys so much of our inner selves
Though, if we touch each other's spirit
Perhaps then life that exists after death
Can revolve around our inner spirit
And we can, and will ignore the slights
And hurts inflicted upon us by people not
Accepting that we never die, simply move
On to another level of God's wonderment.

Living in America Today

We're here to take your home.
Foreclosure we call it. Makes us
Forget you'll be homeless. Not
Quite the dream you had when we
Said here you are, you can afford it.

Pack up the dreams, sell the lawnmower.
Where do we go from here? Live in the car.
Why not, we are only the foreclosure men,
We don't care, only doing our job - lady.

Is this the America of the Thirties?
Nope, only problem is it's 2011.
Back to shanty town living.
Pick the paper out of the trash.

Read 43% on welfare.
Where do we go from here? Government relief.
We are not losers who choose not to work.
We are 'the people' politicians
Begged for our vote.

Now the dream has died, we can only bury it,
And move on to God knows where. Listen do
You hear the now being spoken,
Is it the new deal?

Fat chance, no stimulus here,
Bankers won't lend to the people.
The now is the same old rhetoric.
We haven't a chance against the fat cats of avarice.

Rolling Stone

On this long road to nowhere
Meeting folk going my way
I can't seem to find the time
To keep friends in my mind.

Trying to understand how I ended up
Staring at distant horizons,
Wondering why they're receding
In the rear view mirror.

It's only me everyday on the winding
Rolling road, knowing there is
No arrival, just traveling on.

Finding out the long, winding road is
Littered with regrets, though here I am
Still rolling along looking towards that
Far distant horizon knowing
It's an illusion, I'm going nowhere.

I'm back where I started,
Seems only yesterday I left
Looking for a destination.

Mall

Mall, store lined, one or the other stating
Massive sale ends today.

Perhaps a way to bring us in and be at peace
They simply say: last five days.

Declaring: no profit left.
30% of, 75% of... why not give it away?

Make an offer!
Diamond sale!

Go on give's one...
Are you insane?
This is a diamond sale.

Not a red carpet moment.
Walk on by, cold tiles underfoot.

As cold as the greeting
Stating 30% or 75% of.

All it's saying is
Buy, buy, Buy. Bye.
OKAY.

The Old Street's Gone

Terraced rows of caring people dispersed.
You'll be all right up the road, these old streets
Only slums where God fearing, hard working people live.

Don't worry, we're only knocking down your lives.
Only thing is you won't know that until it is too late.
Up the road you'll have all the niceties you want.
None of your needs, they are left in, rubble razed tumbled homes.

Short 5 and 6 blocks of lovely locked down uncaring terraces
The odd set of semidetached thrown in to break the monotony.
Caring people left bewildered by the sudden growth of needy children.
After all they have all their wants, anything they need they steal.
What has happened to the Good working class God fearing people?

We moved up the road might as well be the moon, such an alien place
Who are these children of ours running wild when they have all their wants?
They have the entire world I wish I still had mine. Down the road, living,
When all we talked about and hoped for was for a better tomorrow.
Look around and wish they had never gone away, locked in, tied down by fear
Of the crime. You get what you wish for, only this time it won't be those
Terraced rows of caring, sharing, God fearing people
Living in tumble down terraced homes down the road.

Australia

Land of beauty, land of colour,
Land that lies way down under.
Flag of yellow, black, and red
Its people indigenous to the land
Called Australia, lying way down yonder.

Modern cities, bush and country,
Colour and light its main delight.
Cross its red heartland, it's a land
You'll never get over, this land called
Australia, a handshake, a nod.

This land harbours all people, asks
Only that you accept their way of life.

Here it is great Southern Land,
Vibrant and proud
Pack a swag, go, walk around.
It's a hard life, a good life, no handouts,
This is a land called Australia.

The Fool

His actions imply simplicity.
Though when we look
Beyond the alleged absurdities
We discover many complexities lie hidden
Beneath, the fools play, acting.
Gets him through his working day and relationships.

Never reveals himself to anyone, not even himself.
A jester one moment then, bewildering
To all, he becomes the hidden man.
Down, way deep down his many talents
Never revealed. Quickly thinks - hide,
Play the fool, can't let anyone in, wouldn't do,
People might get to know, I'm not the fool they see.

Many actions the fool observes in people.
Knows they are hiding, he is nobody's fool, can see
Keen minds hiding from themselves.
Let's play the fool, easier, softer way, no one
Shall know me. Even when I hold my head up high
And walk with you, talk with you, never shall you
See anyone except the man you perceive as the fool.

Strolling... in the Car

We wandered over hill and dale
Exhaust fumes catching in our throats
As we noted the people out walking
In their cars

Dipping beams to greet other casually
Strollers out to take the morning fumes,
All strolling in their cars

Occasionally come across one of those
Strange breed, you know the sort, want to
Perambulate along lane ways enjoying
The morning smells of hedgerows,

And watching
Small birds flit daintily about,

Whilst we in our cars sit, walking,
And laugh out loud knowing
Our exhaust fumes have ruined their morning

Motorized walking in the morning
Makes one wonder what happened to
Old way of strolling, now everyone
Is rolling past, letting us enjoy the exhaust fumes

Killing Time

We wonder where it goes,
Where it flows, this enigma
Called time.

One moment that callow youth,
Then suddenly, as if awakened
From slumber, we stare down the years

Noting the good and bad times are all
Distant memories lying fallow in our mind.
Yesterday's time demanded respect, instead

We spent time, killing time, never believing
That time would kill us. All we can do is
Accept ourselves, and strive to be
The best we can be. In the remains of time.

Memories - There and Back

We're here and, well, we were there.
Many a mile travelled on this road.
Okay, let's see, do I remember what
The old used to be, the if only and maybe?
The many moments we let slide away?

Always thinking - okay, if I hit a wall I'll
Breach it. Now this wall I'm at is layered in
Memories, no way through, each brick a thought,
Each course a moment in time, each held
Together and kept apart by the cement of time,
Bondage to dreams of old used to be.
Gotta stop travelling this road of yesterdays.

Here we are, and here we stay contented and
Happy on the road of today, went many a place
And now, glancing back, don't regret. I'll put my
hand on the wall and recover old times, old friends
forgotten in the mists of yesterdays.

Come Around Again

Haven't seen you around much
You're here to say you love me,
Wouldn't hurt to tell a lie, help me to
Accept that you only come around when
You want, and need a bit of loving.

Okay, here we are, on the carousel of lies.
Let's hear the new one, the reason,
You're back in town, been awhile since
You were here, same Old Street,
Same old strife and here you are knocking
On my life, is to be you and me fighting
On the street, don't think so, not this time.

Okay, can't say it's good to see you, you'll give me
What I don't want, rage, anger, hurt and despair,
Let's just stay apart, that way I'll still have my heart,
It's been way too long, haven't had you on my mind.
Listen, don't come around again, let me forget you.
Just the thought of you freezes my heart, this is my life
And you're not pulling it apart.

Random Man

Wandering through this repressed land
I find myself living as a random man -
No place worth stopping, no place
Worth going to, just another
Rolling stone trying to survive
On life's lengthy highway.

Looking into garbage bags
Grab hold of a can, don't let go, it's all
This random man has, other people's
Food in this lost land, used to be
A worthwhile man then the bankers
Changed our lives stripped us of all we had
Now I wander, no home, no hearth.

I hear the clamour of voices at night
Claiming it'll be alright though I
Can't see an end in sight, believe I will
End up as a wandering random man.
Only thing I have left is to be the best I can.

An Inoffensive Man

Quiet man, nobody noticed him,
Totally inoffensive. Would laugh,
Be stoic when required, just be there
When needed, not noticed, simply around.
Lived quietly trying to do no wrong.

People can't see inoffensive men, prefer
The insecure loud mouth oaf, he's always
Out there with unwanted opinions, pushing,
Always needing to be noticed whilst the quiet man
Gets on with it not needing attention, cause
And effect affected by his quiet actions. The world
Only sees the braggart shouting offensively.

All the while the inoffensive man moves on, doesn't
Stand around waiting to be noticed, just puts things
In motion year after year always around, there when
Needed although goes 'unnoticed', his way of living.
Quiet, inoffensive, full life giving not taking, unlike
The loudmouthed insecure aggressive braggart
Screaming - I'm here, see me, I need, I need to be noticed.

Here We Go Again Running Away

From the bogey men on the 12th day.

Well, we all call it going on holiday
But really we're just running down that old
Hoary road of digging in, hoping it will all go away.

Problem is whist we are running, others
Have created a plantation, when we stop running
What have we got, not a lot - all owned by the planters.

Let's stop running, plant a little bit of grass for ourselves,
We don't get a lot of room to get about in, we call this
Our land. No, you can't, we planted that bit a long time ago,
Plantation owners not liking assertion of rights.

Problem is there's no one to turn to. Nobody can help
We're out on that treadmill running, running,

Going on holiday, the other are entrenched
Not for moving, declaring No Surrender,
We shall not be moved, and here we are
On holiday from the plantation owners.

Hard Rain

A hard rain keeps falling,
Lost hopes and dreams scrawling
Around, inside crumbling homes.
It's a hard acid rain.

This perfect storm caused by greed
All us played a part small or large.
The hard rain descends battering lives
Nothing to shield or protect us.

Our livelihood swept the way of all,
Promises built on shaky ground,
Our lives are lost in the storm
Drains of our cities.

This hard rain gonna keep on falling,
No way out, no easy solutions, only poverty
And what used to be called third world living.

We grabbed at straws, ended up holding
The short straw of no hope, all we got is a
Hard hard rain and it's never stopping.

In Our Time

We are Australian
And in our time we are asked
To go over there, now living here
And not over there, we need to ask
A simple question: *WHY* should we
Go over there?

In Afghanistan in our time all is as ever was,
A continuous war, do we want, do we need to
Be over there, where is over there?
Vietnam or Afghanistan.
In Australia this land is where
We are needed, to protect and serve our
Country, we remember other lands and
The hard fought wars.

What did we ever get for going over there?
Our men died, were disabled and soon forgotten.
Not even a pat on the back for going over there,
Another last post sighs across this our land
Called Australia, *LEST WE FORGET*
Our destiny lies with our loved ones here,
Not over there in the dust of Afghanistan.

Infant in Me

The infant in me knows no sorrow,
I have only my tomorrows, no corners,
Hiding in my mind the thoughts I have yet to
Know, all my dreams are held in my mother's
Arms but then that's only the infant in me.

Walk, stand, balance, all beyond my control
Yet I know that will happen, I shall walk, run,
Stand alone when I have lost the infant in me.
No hurry to get those worries, gonna roll
Down many a long road when I have lost
That happy child, the infant in me just losing
Out to time, and here I am running out of control.

Grown out of that infant mind, now all I have are
The sorrows of growing into adulthood, wishing
I was holding on tight to my mother's arms again,
All my sorrows dealt with, grown old in body but
The strength of me is the infant in me.

The Quiet People

Table set for tea, asking
Where are the children?
They're out shooting at
The Brits. Don't be stupid,
Army got guns, Prods got guns,
Ain't no other guns in Ballymurphy.

That's what we're told, all the dead
People had guns even Father Mullan.
Now they must have had guns, paras
Shot them dead, if they hadn't guns
Then why where they shot? Government men
Said shoot the Fenian bastards, and the army
Said okay execute them, and claim they had guns.

Easy. They're Catholics, nobody cares.
Forty years on and still we are told
They all had guns.
Only the Army had guns, Prods had guns.
People of Ballymurphy hadn't got guns.
Forensic proved the people had no guns.

Then why were they murdered? A well
Internment, illegal act - might as well be hung
For a sheep as a lamb, and they were all lambs
Slaughtered by the British Army.
The blood of innocence bloomed bright as
A sunburst on the pavements of
Ballymurphy that heinous day in August 1971.
We, the quiet people,
Want an apology. 'None forthcoming'.

www.ingramcontent.com/pod-product-compliance
Lightning Source LLC
La Vergne TN
LVHW051649080426
835511LV00016B/2570